Self Publishing

How to Write, Publish and Sell Your Own Children's Book

S.A. Knight

Chapter 1-Getting Started

If you have always thought of being a writer but felt that you didn't know what to do or where to start, or maybe you just thought that getting a book published was just too expensive you can live your dreams by writing your book, and then publish it on your own. Years ago, you had to spend thousands of dollars to publish a book. Today, you can cut costs and self-publish your own work for very little money out of your pocket. I have written three children's books in two months using this method of writing and have barely used any money to do it. I am going to let you in on all the little things that I have learned along the way; you don't have to sit in on webinars that are going to cost you hundreds of dollars to basically learn what I am going to explain to you here in this book. This is going to help make the task of writing and publishing your book a lot easier. Since writing children's books is my favorite genre, I am going to mainly focus on children's books. So, grab a notebook and a pen, and let's get started!

Chapter 2 – Research

Research is one of the most important parts of the writing process. To write your book, you are going to have to do some research. You want to do research to make your book seem more authentic and well written. Nothing is worse than writing a book where you get facts, dates and other information wrong. ("Profitincome.biz") Researching different types of books that have been successful in the genre that you have chosen for your book is imperative. You can use your library and the Internet to do research. I like to do research on what I am writing before I start writing my book, I start by making a list of everything I know about the subject that I am writing about, and then I research more about the subject to learn more and to make sure that all my facts are correct. The internet makes it easier to do research now more than ever. You can go online to find all the information that you need for your book.

An excellent book has the following:

Three-dimensional, believable characters

>A conflict

>A climax

>A resolution to the conflict

You need to have some conflict in the book right from the start, and that conflict has to solved before you get to the end of your book. It does not mean that your book has to have a happy ending, but you have to make sure that all the conflict is solved, and you can't leave anything hanging. You also want to make your book in a way that the climax builds up throughout the book. You also need to decide what point of view you will use for your book. First person narrative is easier to write and is limited to the thoughts and actions of the main character or narrator of the story. You can write your book from a first person observant, which tells the story from another character's point of view which is observing the action. You can choose the third person and still write from the point of view of the main protagonist.

If you decide to write from the third person perspective, you can reach into the point of view from other characters in the book. Of all styles of writing, third person omniscient, which sees into the heads of all the characters is the most difficult to write. Take a look at books that you like to read and see which writing style will best fit your book. Most books written are in the past tense, and you will have to decide if you are going to write in the present tense or the past tense.

⁇ ⁇

Chapter 3 - Completing the First Draft

You can start writing your first draft after you have done your research and have decided what kind of book that you want to write. This can change as you go along, although most of the information you write will be used in your final draft. It is best to write everything that comes to mind down first because this will help you to brainstorm and may help to get your book going in the direction that you want it to. I chose children's books as my genre because writing for younger children is easier and faster than writing a novel for older kids. When making children's books, I start with researching what is selling in the marketplace. Go over to Amazon and do some searching to see what is selling and what people want to read and buy. Start by making a title for your book, Next, make a list of characters that you want in your book; you can add to any of this (or take away from this as you go along) but it may help you to come up with some ideas. I also make a numbered list of what I wish to happen in my book (a numbered list based upon book scenes).

For me, it is a much easier to start a template to get my book started. I type mine out on a word document and save it in a .doc or .docx file. You may also want to add a description of your book. All of these things make the writing process easier and helps you to brainstorm and stay organized. Here is an example of a book that I have written, just to give you an idea of how I went about my template:

Title: Pablo Gets Glasses

What is happening in my book: Pablo's having a bad day at school, his teacher moved his seat to the back of the classroom, and now Pablo can't see the chalk board. Join Pablo as his mother takes him to the eye doctor for an eye exam and a new pair glasses. This child friendly book is rich in creative full- color images that are sure to capture your child's attention and build imagination, all while teaching a valuable lesson on why it's important to not tease others.

Characters: Pablo the Panda

Patty Panda (Pablo's Mom)

Mrs. Wendy (Pablo's teacher)

Billy Bear (A boy in Pablo's classroom)

Dr. Beary- Eye Doctor

Series of Events that will occur in my book

1) Pablo goes to school and can't see the chalk board Pablo

2) Pablo and his mom visit the eye doctor

3) Pablo gets an eye exam

4) Pablo gets glasses

5) Pablo goes to school and Billy bear makes fun of Pablo's new glasses

6) Pablo feels very sad

7) Mrs. Wendy tells Billy and the rest of the class why it's not nice to make fun of others

8) Billy bear feels bad and apologizes to Pablo

9) Pablo can see the board clearly

10) Pablo goes home and tells his family about his day- everyone is happy.

If you want to see images that I got from an amazing illustrator from Fiverr for my book you can go here:

http://www.amazon.com/Pablo-Gets-Glasses-S-Knight-ebook/dp/B01BW83CAI/ref=sr_1_1?ie=UTF8&qid=1458256810&sr=8-1&keywords=pablo+gets+glasses

My book is free for Kindle Unlimited users.

Chapter 4 – Finding an Illustrator and Outsourcing

Great! So you did your research and have an outline template of your book. Now, it's time to look for an illustrator to make some fabulous pictures for your book. I Use Fiverr to find graphic illustrators that make great illustrations for my children's book; After I have completed my list template, I send that template to the illustrator that I picked on Fiverr and asked them if they can make illustration's for every number that I have listed on my template (ask your illustrator will make pictures for you numbered series of events that will happen in your book) , and usually all rights to pictures are included (make sure to ask your illustrator if all the copyrights for your drawings are included, so you can use your illustrations any way you want). Don't be afraid to shop around for the best deal, if you send your template over to an illustrator and you don't like what kind of deal you get, keep looking around there are plenty of illustrators to pick from. I usually pay $5 for each illustration; some illustrators on Fiverr will charge you extra for copyrights. For my Pablo book, I payed a total of $50 for all ten illustrations, and that even included the cover and copyrights. I always write my template, send it to an illustrator and then write my book after I get my illustrations back, for me it's a lot easier to get my book done after I see my illustrations.

Since you are a new writer, the easiest way to make a cover for your book is on Createspace, they have a really cool cover creator that you can upload the picture your illustrator drew. Or if you do not have a cover picture from your illustrator, you can make your own cover; try Canva.com I make most of my covers myself and Canva makes it really easy and fun.

I like to correct mistakes as I go along, sometimes having someone else read over your book is a good idea. It's always nice to get opinions from others; you can join groups for new writers on Facebook to get some honest opinions about your writing. Look online for a grammar checker that checks for plagiarism (I like Grammarly.com because you can check for all errors and it also helps you to correct sentence fragments and checks for plagiarism) If you feel unsure of your book, you can also go to Fiverr.com and hire a proofreader for $5. You can even hire a Ghostwriter at Fiverr to do ALL your work of writing for you. Hiring a Ghostwriter is an excellent choice for someone who can't write or has trouble putting their ideas to paper, plus you can get a book written and published fast and start making royalties from those books.

Although with writing children's books, you don't have to worry much about plagiarism because your research is going to mainly consist of looking at what is selling in the market place.

Chapter 5 - Finding a Self Publisher Online

It is a good idea for new writers to self- publish their own books, and then market it themselves. You can use self-publishers that print to order and do not charge large publishing fees. Your book will be given an ISBN number (you can get it through Createspace for no cost) and it will then be listed on places like Amazon, where most people today are buying books. The author can have their book in a bookstore as long as it has an ISBN.

Self-publish your book with a publisher that does print to order publishing will get you more profits, and you don't have to spend any money to do it with Createspace, and your book will be listed online for those who are interested in buying it.

 Createspace is my favorite publishing platform. Here you just sign up for an account; start by hitting the "add new title" button, and then the rest is very easy , just follow the first three steps by adding your title, choose paperback, and then follow the guided step by step process. You will upload your word document file to Createspace and they will format it for you, so no worries; Createspace will convert your word document to a PDF file. You will also be asked if you want to submit your book as an eBook on KDP (Amazon's Kindle Platform) I always do because you can get a lot more buyers for your book when they can just quickly download a copy on Amazon. That is what makes Createspace so fantastic, you can publish your paperback and have eBooks that are ready for download on Amazon. Another great thing about using Createspace is that you can easily use their online cover creator (super easy just follow step by step instructions) to make great covers for your book; just make sure you get pictures from public domains. I use Pixabay.com and Openclipart.com to get free images to use for my covers and books. You can also use Google: click on images, then click on usage rights, and then make sure to hit "labeled for reuse and modification." Those are the pictures that can be used freely. You may also want to consider enrolling in KDP Select, where people can download your book from the Kindle library, and you will get paid royalties from their large global fund; another great way to increase sales of your book. The only thing about KDP Select that you have to be aware of is that while you are enrolled in the KDP Select program, you can't have your digital downloads available on any other platforms. After some time in the KDP Select program, I drop out of the program so that I can list my digital downloads on other platforms like Nook press, and iTunes.

 Another self-publishing platform that you may be interested in is Lulu.com; they are print on demand, which means that you do not have to order a lot of books, they will print them as they are ordered and you get the difference of the cost to produce the book to the cost that it is selling for. On LuLu, you can use their tools to make sure that your book is formatted correctly. For LuLu, you have to submit your file in a PDF format, and here you can also get your book in either a hardcover or paperback. A

plain book cover with lettering you can have done for you for

about $200. Your book will then be available to purchase on

LuLu, and you can also have it listed on Amazon.

There are now many choices available for those who want to

self-publish their books. Because of internet technology and

computer technology, it is easy for any writer to get their book

published through self-publishing.

Chapter 6-Your Book Is Printed - Now What?

Congratulations! You are now an author and ready to start to promote your book. There are many ways that you can promote your book both online and off. One thing that you will want to do is to promote your book by getting some positive reviews on Amazon. Join some authors groups online; check on Facebook there are many authors groups. You can find other new writers that will be more than happy to give you a review on your book; in return you can review their book. Ask family members to download a copy and give you a positive review. The more reviews it gets, the better it will be on Amazon.

You should have a website to advertise your work; you can link your website to go back to Amazon where people can purchase your books. You can also sign up to become an affiliate of Amazon and get paid a commission on all of your sales. You can also look up book review websites and ask to have your book reviewed online, and you can place a link to your book. Open up a page on your Facebook and you can promote your books here at a low cost. I use this often because for $20 you can boost one of your posts for three days, and you can reach some 3,000 people I notice that when I do this that I will get an increase in sales. Use other social networks like Twitter and Instagram to get your book out there. I have also used sites such as Craigslist to advertise free.

Take advantage of all the ways to promote your book online; you can find a lot of sites where you can post about your book. Most books today are sold primarily online. Go to Digg.com and talk about your book, have friends and family go on and mention your book. You can use a Yahoo site called Propeller; that is something like Digg, anyone who has a Yahoo account can talk about a book. If you get enough buzzes about your book, it can appear on the Yahoo homepage. You need to get as much exposure online that you can for your book; this is how you get your name out there and increase sales.

Book signings are another great way to get some exposure to your book; you can call your local bookstores and ask about the book signing and bring books to sell. Call local schools and see if you can read your book in the class, and a week before you go, you can drop off order slips to the school for the teacher to pass out to the children so that they can order books.

If you want to have your books for sale in larger bookstores, you have to go to the main office and give them a copy, and they will let you know if they want to order from you. Although this may be time consuming, it is very well worth a try you have nothing to lose.

Try to find book fairs that cater to new authors; you can make bookmarks for your book to be handed out at these fairs. Be sure to put all your information on the bookmarks such as your website, the name of your book and a link where people can go on and purchase your book. The more you promote your book, the more interest it will generate. If you have wanted to write a book but are not sure if you can get a publisher, you should consider self-publishing your book.

Go online and take a look at the following sites:

www.Createspace.com

www.lulu.com

www.kdp.amazon.com

These are the most popular sites online for self-publishing. Take a look at their frequently asked questions and rates to see which is right for you. Then get started writing and make your dream a reality!

Sites to Consider For Self Publishing

www.Createspace.com

www.Lulu.com

www.kdp.amazon.com

www.nookpress.com

www.itunesconnect.apple.com

www.ingramspark.com

Sites for getting FREE Images:

www.openclipart.com

www.pixabay.com

www.publicdomainimages.org

www.google.com (click on images, than search tools, than usage

rights...make sure you click on "labeled for reuse with modification")

Sites for Advertising and Promoting your book

www.Digg.com

www.propeller.com

www.Facebook.com

https://www.facebook.com/groups/177830275661611/

https://www.facebook.com/groups/advertisingbooks/

Amazon Books, Likes and Rankings:

https://www.facebook.com/groups/443014452450161

Amazon Kindle Book Sharing Club:

https://www.facebook.com/groups/kindlebooksharingclub/

Asking for eBook reviews on Amazon:

https://www.facebook.com/groups/238409906321951/

Writers and Authors Publicity:

https://www.facebook.com/groups/154804701390698/

To Promote Books for Children:

https://www.facebook.com/groups/BooksForChildren/

https://www.facebook.com/groups/childrenbookclub/

Children's eBook Club:

https://www.facebook.com/groups/1402168653333862/

Get Barnes & Noble and Amazon reviews for your book:

https://www.facebook.com/groups/329297977202165/

Great to make covers for your book

www.canva.com

www.Adobephotoshop.com

Don't forget, you can make amazing covers for your book at
Createspace after you upload your file, and it's easy peasy! This is the
best way to go for newbies!

Site to find Illustrators, Proofreaders and just about anything you need

www.Fiverr.com

www.Elance.com

www.Odesk.com

www.Guru.com   (A great place to find someone to Ghostwrite all
your work)

Thank You for purchasing this book. I hope the information that I gave you is helpful and makes the writing process easier for you. Use the template and fill in your information about your book, find an illustrator on fiverr and have the illustrator make some awesome illustrations. After you see your illustrations you will be able to put your children's book together fairly easily. Upload the word document of your book to Createspace (after you uploaded your transcript to Createspace, you will be asked if you want to upload your transcript to KDP, I always do because Createspace is for paperback books and when you sell on Amazon, you want to also offer your book in digital format to). I make most of my money on digital downloads. Make the best out of all the free places there are to advertise your book, social media is a great free way to advertise your book.

Most of all have fun writing your book! Keep writing... and enjoy all the royalties you see rolling in every month. Good luck to you!

Works Cited

"Self Publishing - Discover How to Write ... - Profit

Income." Insert Name of Site in Italics. N.p., n.d. Web. 17 Mar.

2016 <http://profitincome.biz/self_publishing.html>

www.ingramcontent.com/pod-product-compliance
Lightning Source LLC
Chambersburg PA
CBHW072027280526
45788CB00007B/2701